TUNISIA 2016 HUMAN RIGHTS REPORT

EXECUTIVE SUMMARY

Tunisia is a constitutional republic with a multiparty, unicameral parliamentary system and a president with powers specified in the constitution. In October 2014 the country held free and fair parliamentary elections that resulted in the Nida Tounes (Call of Tunisia) Party winning a plurality of the votes. Nida Tounes formed a coalition government with the Islamist party Nahda and several smaller parties. On July 30, parliament withdrew confidence from Prime Minister Habib Essid, and President Beji Caid Essebsi appointed Youssef Chahed prime minister on August 3. Parliament approved a new government on August 27 with 26 ministers and 14 state secretaries.

Civilian authorities maintained effective control over the security forces.

The most significant human rights problems included slow and opaque investigations and prosecutions of alleged security force human rights abuses; arbitrary arrests and detentions of suspects under antiterrorism laws; and the infringement of gay, lesbian, bisexual, transgender, and intersex (LGBTI) rights.

Other human rights problems included physical abuse of prisoners in detention centers and prisons, poor prison and detention center conditions, lack of judicial independence, lax prosecutorial environment with poor transparency, violence against journalists, corruption, gender-based violence, and societal obstacles to full economic and political participation of women.

The government took steps to investigate officials who committed abuses, but investigations into police, security force, and detention center abuses lacked transparency and frequently encountered long delays and procedural obstacles.

Section 1. Respect for the Integrity of the Person, Including Freedom from:

a. Arbitrary Deprivation of Life and other Unlawful or Politically Motivated Killings

Security forces reportedly used excessive force that resulted in the killing of civilians. In its 2015 report, the Tunisian Organization Against Torture (OCTT) noted that cases of torture and mistreatment represented 90 percent of all reported

abuses by security forces. Seven percent of the cases were suspicious death under detention, 2 percent were rape, and 1 percent was unlawful detention.

On August 20, 23-year-old Hamed Sassi was reported dead in Mornag prison. According to the Observatory of Rights and Freedoms in Tunisia, images of his body showed clear signs of torture. Sassi had been held in Mornag prison since November 2015. Sassi's mother reported the family was prevented from visiting Sassi while in prison and they were not informed of his illness or hospital treatment prior to his death. The general prosecutor launched an investigation at the court of first instance of Ben Arous, which remained pending.

The army, police, and National Guard suffered 111 fatalities and more than 230 injuries in repeated attacks by terrorist groups since 2011. During the year terrorist groups killed 20 security force members, including 13 during an attack on Ben Guerdan on March 7, four in Tatouine on May 11, and three on August 31 in Kasserine.

Media and civil society organizations reported the deaths of several individuals in detention. In 2015 the family of Abderaouf Kridis accused the police station of al-Medina al-Jadida of refusal to implement the court order and neglecting Kridis' psychological condition, as well as failing to inform them of his transfer to hospital and subsequent death in August. Kridis was in al-Mornaguia prison pending a court hearing after he stabbed his neighbor. The court had earlier granted his mother a judicial warrant to commit him to a psychiatric facility for treatment for psychological problems. A spokesperson for the General Directorate of Prison Services told media that the office launched an investigation into the case. Kridis' lawyer confirmed that the investigation continued, and no results were available at year's end.

b. Disappearance

There were no reports of politically motivated disappearances.

c. Torture and Other Cruel, Inhuman, or Degrading Treatment or Punishment

Although the law prohibits such practices, police reportedly subjected many detainees to harsh physical treatment, according to first-hand accounts provided to international organizations. Several prominent local human rights lawyers decried the practice of torture in police stations and detention centers. Human rights nongovernmental organizations (NGOs) criticized the government for reluctance to investigate torture allegations. The French NGO Action by Christians for the Abolition of Torture, in collaboration with three local human rights associations, detailed the dysfunctional mechanisms for complaining of torture during custody, detention, and imprisonment in a January 2015 report entitled *Justice in Tunisia: Year Zero*. In April the UN Committee Against Torture reviewed the country's record on torture and other cruel, inhuman, or degrading treatment or punishment. The committee noted progress in addressing issues of torture and abuse but cited concerns with the application of the antiterrorism law, the appearance of impunity for abusers, forensic evidence as proof of sexual acts, and reports of attacks against human rights defenders. The government stated it prepared a guidebook on the prevention of torture for prisons, detention centers, and the judicial system and provided training for judges and other law enforcement personnel on the content.

In July the OCTT reported that Aymen Rahani, imprisoned since 2014, was tortured and assaulted by prison guards, which led to his loss of sight in one eye. His family filed a suit at the general prosecutor's office demanding investigation. Results of the investigations were pending. The same NGO reported in February that 18-year-old student Wael Boualagui, imprisoned since 2015, informed his family that prison guards had repeatedly assaulted him and that he was the victim of two attempted rapes. Boualagui reportedly did not identify the perpetrator of the assaults due to of fear of retribution. He also alleged that prison officials forced him to take medication against his will, which he claimed resulted in the loss of control of his hand.

According to an OCTT report released on May 10, an investigative judge issued an arrest warrant during the year against two police officers for verbally and physically abusing Ahmed ben Abdi when they stopped him in the street in 2013. Ben Abdi was physically assaulted in a police car when he was arrested. The two officers remained in pretrial detention at year's end.

Prison and Detention Center Conditions

Prison and detention center conditions were below international standards, principally due to overcrowding and poor infrastructure.

Physical Conditions: Prisons were understaffed and lacked adequate equipment to deal with the number of inmates. Overcrowding persisted, despite periodic amnesties since the 2011 revolution, due at least in part to the transfer of a large number of prisoners from 14 prisons damaged during prisoner uprisings in 2011.

The UN Office of the High Commissioner for Human Rights, in a 2014 report, cited overcrowding and poor infrastructure as the biggest problems in prisons. The highest rates of overcrowding were found in four prisons: Kasserine (151 percent), Kairouan (138 percent), Mesadine Prison of Sousse (116 percent), and Jendouba (114 percent). The report concluded that conditions often forced inmates to share beds.

In May the Tunisian League for Human Rights (LTDH) published a report that criticized prison overcrowding and unsanitary conditions. It claimed space allotted for Tunisian inmates averages 22.6 square feet per person, well below the 43 square feet recommended by international norms. The report also noted that many detention centers were well over capacity, citing the center in Kairouan, which was at 300 percent of capacity.

As of September there were an estimated 21,350 prisoners and detainees, of whom 10,220 were convicted prisoners and 11,130 were in pretrial detention. The high percentage of pretrial detainees, which stemmed from case-flow problems, raised concerns about the capacity of the courts to dispense timely justice.

The law requires pretrial detainees to be held separately from convicted prisoners, but the Ministry of Justice reported that overcrowding forced it to hold pretrial detainees together with convicts. Overcrowded conditions were exacerbated by substandard lighting, ventilation, and heating in buildings not originally built to be prisons. Most prisons suffered from decaying infrastructure.

Of the country's 27 prisons, one was designated solely for women, and eight prisons contained separate wings for women.

Detainees at El-Ouardiya, a holding center for migrants awaiting deportation, complained of a lack of legal assistance and medical care at the facility.

Health services available to inmates were inadequate. Very few prisons had an ambulance or medically equipped vehicle. Officials mentioned they lacked equipment necessary for security of guards, other personnel, and inmates. Additionally, there was a lack of adequate training for personnel in crisis management, use of force, and human rights awareness.

Administration: Recordkeeping was inadequate with data not always updated or accurate. During the year officials of the General Directorate of Prisons and

Rehabilitation received training in methods to improve prisoner classification. The directorate developed a new classification system and began updating its database in 2014.

According to prison officials, other problems included lengthy criminal prosecution procedures that led to extended periods of pretrial detention, understaffing at prisons and detention centers, difficult work conditions, and low pay.

Authorities allowed prisoners to receive one family visit per week. Adult prisoners reportedly had some access to educational and vocational training programs, but only a minority had access, due to limited capacity.

Independent Monitoring: The government expanded access to prisons for independent nongovernmental observers, including local and international human rights groups, NGOs, and local media, as well as the International Committee of the Red Cross, the Office of the UN High Commissioner for Human Rights, and the OCTT. In July 2015 the Ministry of Justice and the LTDH signed a memorandum of understanding allowing the league to conduct unannounced prison visits and to issue reports about conditions inside the prisons. After parliament elected members of the Independent National Authority for the Prevention of Torture (INPT) on May 19, the government granted it authority to conduct unannounced inspections of all prisons and detention facilities.

d. Arbitrary Arrest or Detention

The law prohibits arbitrary arrest and detention, although security forces did not always observe these provisions. Human rights organizations expressed concern that the government was using its powers under the state of emergency to place citizens under house arrest with limited evidence or foundation for suspicion.

Role of the Police and Security Apparatus

The Ministry of Interior holds legal authority and responsibility for law enforcement. The ministry oversees the National Police, who have primary responsibility for law enforcement in the major cities, and the National Guard (gendarmerie), which oversees border security and patrols smaller towns and rural areas. Investigations into prisoner abuse lacked transparency and often lasted several months and, in some cases, more than a year.

Civilian authorities maintained control over police, although international organizations, such as Amnesty International and Human Rights Watch (HRW), reported instances of detainees subjected to harsh physical treatment. The government lacked effective mechanisms to investigate and punish abuse, corruption, and impunity by police and prison officials, and there was little transparency in internal investigations. In May a video showing a police officer violently grabbing a young man and another police officer slapping and suffocating him while shouting, "Die, we do not care," spread on social media outlets. Media reported that the young man in the video tried to film the police officers while they were accepting a bribe from a passing driver. The man and a companion were arrested and held in pretrial detention for three days before going to court, where they were accused of verbally abusing the police. The man was sentenced to three months in prison and a 127-dinar fine ($55), while the companion was released. The Tunisian Association Against Torture (TAAT) stated that police had a tendency to resort to violence, and there was a perception of impunity due to lack of adequate investigations and prosecutions. In this case the implicated officers conducted their own investigation, according to TAAT. Ministry of Justice officials acknowledged the need for closer coordination between ministries to address the issue of impunity and more training for security forces.

On August 14, local media reported that the National Guard arrested two police officers in the city of Medenine trying to smuggle tobacco from Libya. One of the police officers had his gun and badge on him; both admitted they had planned to sell the smuggled goods illegally. Both officers were in detention as of November.

Arrest Procedures and Treatment of Detainees

The law requires police to have a warrant to arrest a suspect, unless a crime is in progress or the arrest is for a felony offense. The counterterrorism law, adopted in July 2015, allows for five days of incommunicado prearraignment detention for detainees suspected of terrorism, which can be renewed for two five-day extensions with the court's approval. Arresting officers must inform detainees of their rights, immediately inform detainees' families of the arrest, and make a complete record of the times and dates of such notifications. Police failed at times to follow these regulations and on occasion detained persons arbitrarily. On February 2, parliament approved revisions to the code of criminal procedures in relation to detainee rights. The new law shortens the maximum time of precharge detention for crimes to 48 hours, renewable once by a prosecutor's order, for a maximum of four days. For minor offenses the time limit is 24 hours, renewable once. The law also includes a provision giving the detainee or a family member the right to request the assistance of a lawyer or medical assistance during precharge detention. When police receive the request, they are required to inform the lawyer of the accusations against the client and the time of questioning. Police must notify the lawyer of all interrogations and interactions between the accused and witnesses or victims of the alleged offense and allow the lawyer to be present, unless the accused explicitly waives the right to a lawyer, or the lawyer does not arrive at the prearranged time of questioning.

Detainees have the right to know the grounds for their arrest before questioning and may request a medical examination. The law permits authorities to release accused persons on bail, and the bail system functioned. Detainees can exercise their right to representation by counsel immediately upon detention, and they have the right to counsel during police interrogation, with the exception of terrorism suspects. By law the government provides legal representation for those who cannot afford it, although it was unclear whether the government consistently provided this service. At arraignment the examining magistrate may decide to release the accused or remand the detainee to pretrial detention.

In cases involving crimes for which the sentence may exceed five years or that involve national security, pretrial detention may last six months and may be extended by court order for two additional four-month periods. In cases involving crimes for which the sentence may not exceed five years, the court may extend the initial six-month pretrial detention only by three months. During this stage the court conducts an investigation, hears arguments, and accepts evidence and motions from both parties.

<u>Arbitrary Arrest</u>: Security forces arrested and used force against peaceful demonstrators. Human rights organizations reported instances of arbitrary arrests during an unemployment protest in Tunis on January 22. Borhen Gasmi, a member of the Unemployed Graduates (UDC-Union des Diplomes Chomeurs) and the Popular Front Party, was arrested during the protest and sentenced to 13 months in prison in February. On March 8, the court reduced his sentence to one month, and Gasmi was released on time served. On April 3-4, Ministry of Interior security forces dispersed a sit-in organized by the UDC in Kerkennah in the governorate of Sfax. Police arrested four protesters. On April 12, the Tunisian General Trade Union (UGTT) organized a general strike calling for regional development and the release of the four protesters detained during the sit-in. The LTDH said that in addition to excessive use of tear gas, security forces chased protesters through the streets and in some cases into their homes. The LTDH added that injured protesters could not seek medical treatment due to fear of

retribution and that one of the individuals detained by security forces reported and bore evidence of torture while in custody.

On October 24, HRW reported the use of house arrest for at least 139 persons, leaving many unable to pursue work and studies. HRW interviewed 13 persons, of whom three reported their orders were partially, lifted allowing them to go between home and place of work. Others remained under 24-hour house arrest. There were no clear criteria for partial or 24-hour arrest orders. According to the report, Mohammad Hanachi, unemployed, was summoned to the district police station in Tunis on August 16, where authorities informed him that he was being placed under house arrest and would face imprisonment if he violated the order. He believed the order stemmed from when he was arrested in 2014 and charged with membership in a terrorist organization. After 16 months in prison, a judge in the special terrorism court provisionally released him on February 2. His case was pending.

Pretrial Detention: Pretrial detention remained unpredictable and could last from one month to several years, principally due to judicial inefficiency and lack of capacity. As of early 2016, 58 percent of the 24,000 total inmates were in pretrial status. In a May report, the LTDH criticized the growing number of pretrial detainees, which it said violated human rights and led to overcrowding of prisons.

Detainee's Ability to Challenge Lawfulness of Detention before a Court: Detainees are allowed to challenge the legal bases or arbitrary nature of their arrest. Persons whom the court finds to have been unlawfully arrested or detained will be immediately released upon the decision of the court. Individuals who have been unlawfully detained have the right to request compensation by submitting a request at the court of appeal; however, according to legal groups the procedures for obtaining compensation are complex, and most requests are rejected for failure to meet all required conditions.

e. Denial of Fair Public Trial

The law provides for an independent judiciary. While the government generally respected judicial independence, in one instance it failed to carry out an administrative court decision from 2013 to reinstate 30 of 75 judges dismissed in 2012. Beginning in 2013 a temporary commission began reviewing judicial promotions, transfers, and disciplinary actions. In May 2015 parliament approved a law creating a constitutionally mandated council to replace the temporary body. In June 2015 the constitutional review body ruled the law unconstitutional. In

December 2015 a revised version of the bill was also ruled unconstitutional. In March parliament passed and the president signed a new version of the law. HRW and the Association of Tunisian Judges criticized the law for failing to ensure independence from the executive branch. Elections for members of the new judicial body took place on October 23, which civil society organizations generally praised as fair, transparent, and credible.

Trial Procedures

The law provides for the right to a fair trial, and an independent judiciary generally enforced this right, although defendants complained that authorities did not follow the law on trial procedures consistently. In civilian courts defendants have the right to a presumption of innocence and a public trial. They also have the right to consult with an attorney or to have one provided at public expense, to confront witnesses against them, to present witnesses and evidence, to access government-held evidence, and to appeal verdicts against them. The law stipulates defendants must be informed promptly and in detail of the charges against them, with free interpretation if necessary. They must also be given adequate time and facilities to prepare their defense and not be compelled to testify or confess guilt.

A counterterrorism law passed in July 2015 stipulates that in cases involving terrorism, judges may close hearings to the public. Judges may also keep information on witnesses, victims, and any other relevant persons confidential, including from the accused and his or her legal counsel. The counterterrorism law also extends the amount of time that a suspect may be held without access to legal counsel from five to 15 days, with a judicial review required after each five-day period. Human rights organizations objected to the law for its vague definition of terrorism and the broad leeway it gives to judges to admit testimony by anonymous witnesses.

Military courts fall under the Ministry of Defense. Military tribunals have authority to try cases involving military personnel and civilians accused of national security crimes. A defendant may appeal a military tribunal's verdict and may resort to the civilian Supreme Court. Human rights advocates argued that national security crimes are too broadly defined but acknowledged that, following the 2011 reform of military courts, defendants in military courts have the same rights as those in civilian courts. These include the right to choose legal representation, access case files and evidence, conduct cross-examinations, call witnesses, and appeal court judgments. There is no specialized code for military courts. The law extends the rights related to a fair public trial to all citizens.

Political Prisoners and Detainees

There were no reports of political prisoners or detainees.

Civil Judicial Procedures and Remedies

Citizens and organizations may seek civil remedies for human rights violations through domestic courts, except that military courts handled claims for civil remedies for alleged security force abuses during civil disturbances that occurred during the revolution. Civilian courts heard cases involving alleged abuse by security forces during the year. Some cases did not move forward because security force officials, and occasionally civilian judges, failed to cooperate in the investigations. According to HRW, the lack of provisions criminalizing command dereliction, which would hold senior officers liable for crimes committed by subordinates with explicit or tacit approval, contributed to military courts' light sentences for security force members.

f. Arbitrary or Unlawful Interference with Privacy, Family, Home, or Correspondence

The constitution provides for the right to privacy. The International Commission of Jurists claimed the counterterrorism law extensively infringes on the right to privacy through the use of surveillance. The law allows interception of communications, including recording of telephone conversations, with advance judicial approval for a period not to exceed four months. State agents are subject to a one-year prison sentence if they conduct surveillance without judicial authorization. No complaints were filed against state agents for improper use of surveillance during the year.

Section 2. Respect for Civil Liberties, Including:

a. Freedom of Speech and Press

The constitution and law provide for freedom of speech and press, and the government mainly respected these rights, although there were constraints. An independent press and a functioning democratic political system contributed to an environment generally conducive to these freedoms. Watchdog groups expressed concerns over security forces and other actors committing violence against journalists but noted that the level of violence dropped from the previous year.

Civil society expressed concerns over occasional government interference in media.

<u>Freedom of Speech and Expression</u>: Public speech considered offensive to "public morals" or "public decency," terms undefined in the law, continued to be treated as criminal acts. Provisions of the penal and telecommunications codes, for example, criminalize speech that causes "harm to the public order or public morals" or intentionally disturbs persons "in a way that offends the sense of public decency."

<u>Press and Media Freedoms</u>: The constitution provides for freedom of the press. In August, Tunisia signed the Declaration on Media Freedom in the Arab World, committing the country to principles of media freedom, independent journalism, and the right to information. Activists expressed concern, however, about government interference in media. A 2016 Reporters Without Borders report criticized President Beji Caid Essebsi's speech on January 22, in which he denounced "certain journalists and media" for aggravating unrest during the nationwide employment protests that followed the death of unemployed protester Ridha Yahyaoui. Yahyaoui was electrocuted when he climbed a power pole near the governor's office after the local government removed him from a list of potential candidates for public-sector jobs. The government ordered an investigation into the circumstances surrounding Yahyaoui's death; the case was pending as of November.

On September 26, a military prosecutor charged journalist Jamel Arfaoui with impugning the reputation of the army after he wrote an article published in *Tunisie Telegraph* on July 14 criticizing as inadequate the army's lack of investigation into a military plane crash. On November 16, prosecutors charged Rached Khiari with impugning the reputation of the army and undermining its morale after his participation in a popular talk show during which he claimed that authorities signed an agreement allowing the United States to establish a military base in Tunisia. Both men faced charges of up to three years in prison and were being tried in a military court, although both men were civilians. Khiari faced additional charges of defamation of a civil servant and damaging the morale of the army to harm national defense, which carries a possible death penalty.

<u>Violence and Harassment</u>: Security officials continued to harass and threaten journalists, although to a lesser extent than in 2015, according to human rights organizations. The NGO Tunis Center for Press Freedom (CTLP) reported a decrease in the number of attacks against journalists during the year, to six attacks per month, with the exception of May with 10 reported attacks, mostly by members

of the security forces. Assaults on journalists were mainly reported during summer, when journalists were banned from covering certain festival events in Djerba and Bizerte, according to the CTLP, which called on the Ministry of Interior to open a formal investigation.

<u>Censorship or Content Restrictions</u>: The government penalized individuals who published items counter to government guidelines. While online and print media frequently published articles critical of the government, journalists and activists at times practiced self-censorship to avoid violence targeting journalists, mainly from security forces or other anonymous attackers, according to the CTLP.

<u>Libel/Slander Laws</u>: In July 2015 counterterrorism police summoned Abdelfattah Said for questioning about a video he published on social media expressing his opinions on the cause of the Sousse terrorist attack. He was charged with complicity to facilitate terrorism, defaming a public servant, and knowingly broadcasting false news. Police transferred Said to al-Mornaguia prison in July 2015. In December 2015 the court sentenced Said to one year in prison and a fine of 2,000 dinars ($870). Said's lawyers appealed the decision. According to Amnesty International, there were no further updates on the case during the year.

Internet Freedom

The government did not restrict or disrupt access to the internet, and there were no credible reports that the government monitored private online communications without appropriate legal authority. There was no censorship of websites, including those with pornographic content, with the exception of websites linked to terrorist organizations. According to Internet World Stats, 52 percent of the population used the internet.

Academic Freedom and Cultural Events

There were no reports of government restrictions on academic freedom. The CTLP reported that journalists were banned from some festivals in Bizerte and Djerba.

b. Freedom of Peaceful Assembly and Association

The law provides for the rights of freedom of assembly and association. The state of emergency limited the right of assembly, although the government allowed limited protests to occur. The government did not always respect the right of association.

Freedom of Assembly

The Presidency of the Republic declared several extensions of a nationwide state of emergency, in effect since November 2015, when a suicide bomber attacked members of the Presidential Guard. The most recent extension was issued on October 18 for three months. The government previously ordered extensions of the state of emergency in January after widespread social unrest, in March following a terrorist attack in Ben Guerdan, and in June and July. Protests and clashes with security forces throughout the country started on January 16 in the governorate of Kasserine after the death of Yahyaoui. Local media reported that security forces used violence against protesters and arrested 1,105 persons, including 523 individuals accused of violating a nationwide curfew imposed on January 22.

On April 9, security forces violently dispersed a peaceful group of demonstrators of the General Union of Tunisian Students who were demanding jobs and prohibited them from demonstrating in front of the Prime Ministry.

Freedom of Association

The law provides for the right of freedom of association, but the government did not always respect it. A 2011 law on associations eliminated penalties in the previous law, as well as the prohibition on belonging to, or serving in, an unrecognized or dissolved association. The law eased the registration procedure, making it more difficult for government entities to hinder or delay registration. The International Observatory of Associations and International Development, an independent association that monitors the functioning of civil society, asserted the government was delaying registration of associations through unnecessary bureaucratic hurdles, at times for political reasons, a practice counter to the law on associations.

According to the 2011 law, only the judiciary has the authority to suspend or dissolve an association. According to the Prime Ministry, during the period 2011-16, the government sent warnings to 805 associations and requested the suspension of 234 for violations of the law of associations. Courts suspended 112 of these associations and in four cases ordered the dissolution of the organizations. The Prime Ministry claimed that proper procedure was followed in all cases.

In November 2015 some members of parliament called for the dissolution of LGBTI-focused NGO Shams. On January 4, an administrative court suspended Shams' activities pursuant to a government claim that the association had registered to advocate for the rights of "sexual minorities." The government claimed that the Shams' charter did not allow it to advocate explicitly for gay rights, since the charter only listed the purpose of the organization as advocating for the rights of "sexual minorities." On February 24, an administrative court ruled in Shams' favor, overturning the government's complaint and allowing Shams to function legally; however, the government had not published the organization's charter in the national gazette, leaving Shams unable to register for a bank account or conduct financial activities.

The government issued a ban of the annual conference of Islamist party Hizb Ettahrir scheduled for June 4, citing security reasons. An administrative court overturned the ban on June 3. On the morning of June 4, the governor of Tunis announced the closing of the venue until June 20, using powers granted to him under the state of emergency. The governor told media he took the decision "to avoid disturbing public order." After several warnings to party leaders that the party violated Decree Law 88 of 2011 requiring that associations respect the rule of law and basic democratic principles and are prohibited from calling to violence, hatred, intolerance, or discrimination on a religious basis, the government suspended the activities of Hizb Ettahrir for 30 days beginning on August 15. On August 30, an administrative court overturned the suspension, citing "procedural problems" with the government's case. On September 2, the government brought a criminal case against the party for inciting violence against the state, and the chief prosecutor referred the case to a military court. On September 20, members of Hizb Ettahrir refused to appear before the military court. The case remained pending as of December.

c. Freedom of Religion

See the Department of State's *International Religious Freedom Report* at www.state.gov/religiousfreedomreport/.

d. Freedom of Movement, Internally Displaced Persons, Protection of Refugees, and Stateless Persons

The law provides for freedom of internal movement, foreign travel, emigration, and repatriation, and the government generally respected these rights. The government cooperated with the Office of the UN High Commissioner for

Refugees (UNHCR) and other humanitarian organizations in providing protection and assistance to refugees, asylum seekers, vulnerable migrants, and other persons of concern.

Since 2014 more than 500 individuals complained to the Observatory of Rights and Freedoms of Tunis that the government prevented them from travelling over suspicions of extremism, in some cases apparently based on the travelers' religious attire. The group added that some persons were prevented from travelling despite having a clean record, because they were related to a terrorist suspect. In other cases the observatory claimed that women were prevented from travelling if suspected of prostitution, often based on appearance alone.

Protection of Refugees

Access to Asylum: The country does not have a law for granting asylum or refugee status. Pending the creation of a legal framework, UNHCR is the sole entity conducting refugee status determination. UNHCR provided assistance to registered refugees for primary medical care and in some cases for basic education. The government grants access to schooling and basic public health facilities for registered refugees. When UNHCR ceased providing assistance to the Shousha camp for refugees from Libya in 2013, the camp still housed more than 300 persons who had been denied refugee status. In 2014 the Tunisian Red Crescent counted 98 persons residing in the camp. Of these, 45 were registered refugees who had refused resettlement within the country. The remaining 53 were not granted asylum status and continued to appeal that decision. In October 2014 the government dismantled the Shousha camp; however, UNHCR still provided services to the refugees resettled in homes in Gabes and Medenine. According to press reports, there were approximately 50 refugees and economic migrants still occupying the Shousha camp as of November, the majority of whom were from sub-Saharan countries. UNHCR said that the individuals who chose to remain in the Shousha camp after its dismantlement failed to meet refugee status and fell under the responsibility of the government. According to the Red Crescent, most Shousha occupants turned down temporary housing offered by the government and refused to be regularized in the country. Aid organizations reported that some applied for working papers but had not received a response from the government.

Section 3. Freedom to Participate in the Political Process

The constitution provides citizens the ability to choose their government in free and fair periodic elections held by secret ballot and based on universal and equal suffrage.

Elections and Political Participation

<u>Recent Elections</u>: Citizens exercised their ability to vote in free, fair, and transparent elections in October, November, and December 2014 for legislative and two rounds of presidential elections, respectively.

<u>Political Parties and Political Participation</u>: Of the approximately 170 registered parties, 70 ran electoral lists in the 2014 parliamentary elections. Authorities rejected parties that did not receive accreditation due to incomplete applications or because their programs were inconsistent with laws prohibiting discrimination and also parties based on religion.

<u>Participation of Women and Minorities</u>: Women continued to be politically active but faced societal barriers to their political participation. In a 2011 effort to include more women in the electoral process, the government adopted a candidate gender-parity law requiring political parties to list an equal number of male and female candidates on electoral lists. The law also stipulates male and female candidate names must alternate in order to increase the opportunities for female candidates to be selected.

Section 4. Corruption and Lack of Transparency in Government

The law provides criminal penalties for corruption, and the government took some preliminary steps to implement these laws, although they were not always effective, according to transparency NGOs. In January lawyer and former head of the Tunisian Bar Association Chawki Tabib became the head of the National Commission to Combat Corruption (NCCC). The law tasks the NCCC with investigating and preventing corruption and drafting effective policies to combat corruption. Tabib publicly requested a budget increase to 6.5 million dinars ($2.8 million), claiming the budget was insufficient to address the NCCC's 12,000 backlogged cases of corruption submitted since 2011. In May the government allocated an additional 1.4 million dinars ($608,000) for the NCCC.

<u>Corruption</u>: Anticorruption watchdog groups reported increasing government corruption during the year, especially petty corruption. According to the NCCC, from January to August, 106 cases were referred to the judicial system out of 2,000 received cases. The government referred more than 800 of these dossiers to the NCCC, while complainants themselves directly submitted the remainder of the

cases to the NCCC. The main sectors affected by corruption included real estate, agricultural land, energy, mining, and public procurement.

Financial Disclosure: The constitution requires those holding high government offices to declare assets "as provided by law." At the end of the year, there was no law that requires appointed or elected officials to disclose their income or assets.

Public Access to Information: To improve transparency and promote national reconciliation following the 2011 revolution, a new law granted journalists and civil society organizations access to the records of the previous regime. Bureaucratic hurdles, however, limited the law's implementation. Information from the previous regime deemed sensitive remained inaccessible. The law on transitional justice grants access to this information for members of the Truth and Dignity Commission (TDC), a body established in 2014 and tasked with investigating gross violations of human rights from 1955 until passage of the transitional justice law in 2013.

On March 11, parliament approved a new access to information law that was highly praised by civil society organizations. The new law grants citizens access to documents from public institutions, government agencies, and certain publicly financed associations, and it requires public entities to make information about their offices, including budgets and contact information, publicly available online. The government had one year to implement the program.

Section 5. Governmental Attitude Regarding International and Nongovernmental Investigation of Alleged Violations of Human Rights

A wide variety of domestic and international human rights groups investigated and published without government restriction their findings on human rights cases. Government officials generally were cooperative and responsive to their views.

Government Human Rights Bodies: The government's primary agency to investigate human rights violations and combat threats to human rights is the Ministry of Justice. The High Committee for Human Rights and Fundamental Freedoms is a government-funded agency charged with monitoring human rights. The ministry failed to pursue or investigate adequately alleged human rights violations. The TDC, tasked with investigating human rights violations committed by the state or those who acted in its name, began hearing cases during the year. The deadline for submitting cases to the TDC was June 15, at which time the TDC had received more than 65,000 cases. The TDC held its first public hearings on

November 17. Civil society organizations noted the TDC faced criticism and strong opposition from certain factions of the governing coalition, which could threaten the effectiveness of the commission's work. Observers expressed concerns about the commission's limited financial resources and inability to fill vacant positions.

The INPT was established in 2013 as an administratively independent body. In March parliament selected 16 members for the body. INPT members elected Hamida Dridi as its chair in May. Its members have the authority to visit any prison or detention center to document torture and mistreatment, to request criminal and administrative investigations, and to issue recommendations for measures to eradicate torture and mistreatment. INPT members reported the body faced material and logistical difficulties that prevented it from conducting its work effectively. Human rights organizations praised the election of the board members as a positive step forward. According to HRW, the creation of this new body was "an unprecedented opportunity to address Tunisia's legacy of torture and mistreatment."

Section 6. Discrimination, Societal Abuses, and Trafficking in Persons

Women

Rape and Domestic Violence: Although prohibited by law, rape, including spousal rape, remained a serious problem. The government generally enforced the law against rape. The penal code does not address spousal rape. There was no comprehensive database on the incidence of sexual violence, but NGO groups claimed rape continued to be underreported. Sexual intercourse outside of marriage is illegal, but consensual sex between adults was not prosecuted.

Rape accompanied by the use or threat of violence or threats with a weapon are punishable by death. For other cases of rape, the prescribed punishment is life imprisonment. If the victim is under the age of 20, penalties can be more severe (see section 6, Children). Nonconsensual sexual conduct not meeting the definition of rape, such as sexual assault, aggravated sexual assault, and molestation, may be prosecuted as "indecent assault," which is punishable by up to six years in prison or 12 years if the victim is under the age of 18. In cases of nonviolent sexual assault committed against a minor, charges against the accused will be dropped if the victim's parents consent to marriage, provided the marriage lasts at least two years. Human rights organizations strongly objected to this practice. The punishment is extended to life imprisonment if committed with weapons, threats, or detention or in cases where the victim was mutilated, disfigured, or if the victim's life was endangered. The sentence is five years in prison for "indecent assault" attempted or committed without violence or aggression against a child, which is extended to 10 years if the perpetrator is related to the victim or holds a position of authority over the victim.

Rape remained a taboo and underreported subject. Cultural pressures often dissuaded victims from reporting sexual assault. Convictions for sexual violence were far below the number of actual incidents. A March 2015 study by UGTT's National Commission of Working Women indicated that 32 percent of all women experienced some kind of physical violence, 29 percent experienced psychological violence or harassment, 16 percent suffered sexual violence or exploitation, and 7 percent experienced economic violence, including financial exploitation, extortion, or deprivation of money or the necessities of life. A large portion of violence against women occurred within marriage, according to the study. A 2015 Amnesty International report cited several reasons for underreporting and lack of prosecution for rape and sexual assault, including evidentiary standards that place a high burden on the victim, lack of trust in police and the judicial system, and an inadequate legal definition of sexual assault.

Laws prohibiting domestic violence provide penalties for assault committed by a spouse or family member that are double those of an unrelated individual for the same crime, but enforcement was rare, and domestic violence remained a serious problem.

There were no government public education programs on domestic violence, including rape. Victims received services at two dozen social centers throughout the country. There was a growing demand for services, but social stigma kept many women from utilizing existing resources.

Sexual Harassment: Sexual harassment was a problem, although there was no data to measure its extent. The law requires victims of sexual harassment seeking redress to file a complaint in criminal court, where authorities then investigate the allegations. According to the criminal code, the penalty for sexual harassment is one year in prison and a fine of 3,000 dinars ($1,300). Civil society groups criticized the law on harassment as too vague and susceptible to abuse.

Reproductive Rights: Couples and individuals have the right to decide freely and responsibly the number, spacing, and timing of their children; manage their reproductive health; and have access to the means and information to do so, free from discrimination, coercion, and violence. According to a 2016 study by the *Health and Human Rights Journal*, the country made slow progress in incorporating reproductive rights into its national reproductive health policy. The study highlighted limited accessibility to reproductive health services, low quality maternal health-care services, and discriminatory practices in some regions of the country. The UN Population Fund reported in 2014 that only 10 percent of the primary health-care centers in the northwest, central west and southeast regions of the country provided basic reproductive health services. Family planning had been provided by mobile clinics due to limited infrastructure in rural areas, but recently there was a significant decrease in the number and coverage of these clinics. The World Health Organization reported that single women were discriminated against for treatment of sexually transmitted infections and accessing contraceptives.

Discrimination: The law and constitution explicitly prohibit discrimination based on race, gender, disability, language, or social status, and the government generally enforced these prohibitions. Women faced societal rather than statutory barriers to their economic and political participation. Codified civil law is based on the Napoleonic code, although on occasion judges drew upon interpretations of sharia (Islamic law) as a basis for customary law in family and inheritance disputes.

Newly married couples must state explicitly in the marriage contract whether they elect to combine their possessions or keep them separate. Customary law based on sharia prohibits Muslim women from marrying outside their religion. Sharia requires men, but not women, to provide for their families. Because of this expectation, in some instances sharia inheritance law provides men with a larger share of an inheritance. Some families avoided the application of sharia by executing sales contracts between parents and children to ensure that daughters received shares of property equal to those given sons. Non-Muslim women and their Muslim husbands may not inherit from each other. The government considers all children of those marriages to be Muslim and forbids those children from inheriting from their mothers. Spouses may, however, freely give up to a third of their estate to whomever they designate in their will.

Female citizens can transmit citizenship on an equal basis with male citizens. In November 2015 parliament amended a law that had previously prohibited a mother from traveling outside the country with minor children without written permission from the father. Under the new amendment, there is no discrimination between a mother and father regarding passport application and authorization to leave the country.

The law explicitly requires equal pay for equal work, and the government generally enforced it. The law allows female employees in the public sector to receive two-thirds of their full-time salary for half-time work, provided they have at least one child under 16 or a child with special needs, regardless of age. Qualifying women may apply for the benefit for a three-year period, renewable twice for a maximum of nine years. The government defended the law as allowing women to balance family and professional life, but some women's rights advocates believed treating women and men differently under the law infringed women's rights. Societal and cultural barriers significantly reduced women's participation in the formal labor force, in particular in managerial positions. Women in the private sector earned on average one-quarter less than men for similar work.

Gender-biased Sex Selection: The ratio of boy-to-girl births was 107 to 100. There was no information on any government efforts to address this imbalance.

Children

Birth Registration: Citizenship is derived by birth from one's parents, and the law provides for a period of 10 days to register a newborn. Thereafter, parents have 30 days to explain why they failed to register a newborn and complete the registration.

Child Abuse: A government report cited 601 reported cases of violence against children as of July, triple the number reported in 2013. The Ministry of Women, Family, and Childhood designated 21 psychologists to treat victims and announced its collaboration with civil society to provide increased services for child victims in shelters in Sousse, Sfax, and Tunis. According to the Minister of Women, Family, and Childhood, the rise in the number of reported cases was partially due to an increased willingness of victims to report abuse.

Early and Forced Marriage: The minimum age for marriage for both sexes is 18, but the courts may, in certain situations, authorize the marriage of persons younger than 18 upon the request and approval of both parents.

Sexual Exploitation of Children: The law prohibits child pornography. Anyone who has sexual relations with a girl under age 10 is subject to the death penalty. Anyone who has sexual intercourse with a girl between the ages of 10 and 15 is subject to six years' imprisonment. If the victim is over 15 and under 20, the penalty is five years' imprisonment, unless the individuals are married. The penal code states that if a man has consensual sex with a female minor, he can avoid legal consequences by marrying the victim (see section 6, Women). The country was not a destination for child sex tourism; however, the International Organization for Migration reported some children were victims of sexual exploitation through prostitution, although the extent of the problem was not known.

In July the Ministry of Women, Family, and Children announced that cases involving child victims of violence, which includes sexual abuse, had tripled since 2013. According to data provided by local child protection agencies, instances of recorded abuse increased from 262 in 2013 to 601 as of November. Thirty-three percent of victims of sexual abuse reported direct sexual molestation, while 51 percent reported sexual harassment without direct sexual contact.

International Child Abductions: The country is not party to the 1980 Hague Convention on the Civil Aspects of International Child Abduction. See the Department of State's *Annual Report on International Child Abduction* at travel.state.gov/content/childabduction/en/legal/compliance.html.

Anti-Semitism

An estimated 1,500 Jews lived in the country. In March 2015, vandals destroyed the grave of 18th-century Jewish sage Rabbi Masseoud Elfassi in Tunis. Media reported that motives for the vandalism were unknown but speculated it was the work of looters. After the incident President Caid Essebsi increased security around the cemetery and other Jewish sites and promised a European rabbinical body he would firmly protect the Jewish community and its institutions.

On May 25, an annual Jewish pilgrimage took place on the island of Djerba. Local media estimated participation at 2,000-3,000 persons. The event took place without incident and included the participation of several government ministers. Leaders in the Jewish community and government publicly praised the pilgrimage as a sign of the excellent relationship between the Jewish and Muslim communities.

Trafficking in Persons

See the Department of State's *Trafficking in Persons Report* at www.state.gov/j/tip/rls/tiprpt/.

Persons with Disabilities

The law prohibits discrimination against persons with physical or mental disabilities in employment, education, air travel and other transportation, access to health care, or the provision of other state services. It mandates that at least 1 percent of public- and private-sector jobs be reserved for persons with disabilities. NGOs reported authorities did not widely enforce this law, and many employers were not aware of it. There were no statistics on patterns of abuse in educational and mental health facilities, and individual cases of employment discrimination against persons with disabilities were rarely reported.

Since 1991, the law requires all new public buildings to be accessible to persons with physical disabilities, and the government generally enforced the law. Persons with physical disabilities did not have access to most buildings built before 1991, and most older buildings have still not been made accessible. The government did not ensure access to information and communications.

The Ministry of Social Affairs is charged with protecting the rights of persons with disabilities. The government issued cards to persons with disabilities for benefits such as unrestricted parking, free and priority medical services, free and preferential seating on public transportation, and consumer discounts. The government provided tax incentives to companies to encourage the hiring of persons with physical disabilities. There were approximately 300 government-administered schools for children with disabilities, five schools for blind students, one higher-education school, and one vocational training institution. The Ministry of Social Affairs managed centers in Tunis, Kairouan, Nabeul, and Sfax that provided short- and long-term accommodation and medical services to persons with disabilities who lacked other means of support.

Acts of Violence, Discrimination, and Other Abuses Based on Sexual Orientation and Gender Identity

The law criminalizes sodomy. Convictions carry up to a three-year prison sentence. According to NGOs, authorities occasionally use the law against sodomy to detain and question persons about their sexual activities and orientation, reportedly at times based on appearance alone. LGBTI-focused NGOs reported at least 36 known cases of arrests under the sodomy law as of September, although the government does not keep official statistics on arrests under the law. Human rights organizations and LGBTI-focused NGOs said that police and the courts often ordered men suspected of sodomy to take a rectal exam in order to collect evidence, a practice which human rights organizations and the UN Committee Against Torture strongly denounced.

In December 2015 six men from Rakkada were sentenced to three years each for sodomy, after being forced to undergo a rectal examination. One of the men was sentenced to an additional six months for an "attack on public morals" after police found a video clip on his computer. The court also banished the men from their town for five years following their release from prison. On March 3, a Sousse court of appeals upheld the men's guilty verdict but reduced the sentences to one month and a fine of 400 dinars ($175) each. The judge eliminated the banishment provision. The men told media they had been exposed to sexual abuse and harassment by prisoners and prison guards during their detention.

Associations advocating for LGBTI rights organized campaigns against the criminalization of sodomy and forced medical examinations, which quickly gained popularity on social media and garnered international media attention.

Anecdotal evidence suggested LGBTI individuals faced increasing discrimination and violence, including death and rape threats, although societal stigma and fear of prosecution under sodomy laws discouraged individuals from reporting problems, according to a Euromed report released in September. Due to societal intolerance of same-sex sexual relationships, LGBTI individuals were discreet, and there was no information on official discrimination based on sexual orientation in employment, housing, access to education, or health care, although the Euromed report cited widespread anecdotal evidence of systemic denial of services to LGBTI individuals due to their sexual orientation. LGBTI advocacy work was conducted by several small organizations formed after 2011.

In May several LGBTI associations organized a small, discreet gay pride reception in Tunis. Associations also organized events and public demonstrations to mark the International Day against Homophobia in May.

On April 13, a well-known actor on a popular national television show declared that homosexuality was a "sickness" and said he "despised" gay individuals. Another celebrity repeated these comments publicly soon afterwards. A homophobic social media campaign followed, which included alleged members of security forces posting antigay messages on social media outlets. Several businesses placed signs on their windows refusing service to gay customers. During a Friday sermon on May 3, an imam in Sfax called for gay individuals to be put to death by "throwing them from a high place and stoning them."

Section 7. Worker Rights

a. Freedom of Association and the Right to Collective Bargaining

The law provides workers with the right to organize, form and join unions, and bargain collectively. The law allows workers to strike, provided they give 10 days' advance notice to their federations and receive Ministry of Interior approval. The International Trade Union Confederation and the International Labor Organization characterized the requirement for strike notification as an impediment to freedom of association. The right to strike extends to civil servants, with the exception of workers in essential services "whose interruption would endanger the lives, safety, or health of all or a section of the population." The government did not explicitly stipulate which services were "essential." Authorities largely respected the right to strike in public enterprises and services. The law prohibits antiunion discrimination by employers and retribution against strikers. The government generally enforced applicable laws.

Conciliation panels with equal labor and management representation settled many labor disputes. Otherwise, representatives from the Ministry of Social Affairs, UGTT, and the Tunisian Union for Industry, Commerce, and Handicrafts (UTICA) formed tripartite regional commissions to arbitrate disputes. On January 19, tripartite negotiations led to an agreement on wages in the private sector, which included a 6 percent general wage increase, a 10-dinar increase ($4.50) in the travel allowance, and a three dinar ($1.30) increase for work attendance. Observers generally saw the tripartite commissions as effective, although details on resources available to the commission were unavailable.

Unions rarely sought advance approval to strike. Wildcat strikes (those not authorized by union management) occurred throughout the year but at a level reduced from previous years, according to labor rights organizations. Sector-based unions carried out some strikes and sit-ins, such as those in education and health services and in extractive industries. Even if not authorized, the Ministry of Interior tolerated many strikes if confined to a limited area.

UGTT alleged antiunion practices among private-sector employers, including firing union activists and using temporary workers to deter unionization. In certain industries, such as textiles, hotels, and construction, temporary workers continued to account for a significant majority of the workforce. UTICA, along with the government, maintained an exclusive relationship with UGTT in reaching collective bargaining agreements. The government held organized collective social negotiations only with UGTT. Representatives from the General

Confederation of Tunisian Labor and the Union of Tunisian Labor complained their labor organizations had been ignored and excluded from tripartite negotiations. In June 2015 the administrative court ruled to allow the General Confederation of Tunisian Labor to deduct earnings from paychecks for dues, a right previously allowed only to UGTT. Observers saw the decision as an affirmation of union pluralism in the country.

b. Prohibition of Forced or Compulsory Labor

The law prohibits forced and compulsory labor and provides for penalties of up to 10 years' imprisonment for capturing, detaining, or sequestering a person for forced labor.

The government effectively enforced most applicable codes dealing with forced labor. Some forced labor and forced child labor occurred in the form of domestic work in third-party households, begging, street vending, and seasonal agricultural work (see section 7.c.).

Also see the Department of State's *Trafficking in Persons Report* at www.state.gov/j/tip/rls/tiprpt/.

c. Prohibition of Child Labor and Minimum Age for Employment

The law generally prohibits the employment of children younger than 16. Persons under 18 are prohibited from working in jobs that present serious threats to their health, security, or morality. The minimum age for light work in the nonindustrial and agricultural sectors during nonschool hours is 13. Workers between the ages of 14 and 18 must have 12 hours of rest per day, which must include the hours between 10 p.m. and 6 a.m. Children between the ages of 14 and 16 may work no more than two hours per day. The total time that children spend at school and work may not exceed seven hours per day. The penal code provides for penalties of up to 10 years' imprisonment for capturing, detaining, or sequestering a person for forced labor and up to two years' imprisonment for forced child begging.

Labor inspectors from the Ministry of Social Affairs monitored compliance with the minimum age law by examining the records of employees. The number of inspectors and resources at their disposal lagged behind economic growth. Additionally, according to ministry officials, the labor inspectorate did not have adequate resources to monitor the informal economy fully, officially estimated to constitute 38 percent of GDP. Occasionally, labor inspectors coordinated spot checks with UGTT and the Ministry of Education. According to a 2013 study, 2.6 percent of children under the age of 15 worked, but this figure did not include children who worked in the informal sector, whether as street vendors, beggars, handicraft workers, or seasonal agricultural labor.

Children were subjected to commercial sexual exploitation and used in illicit activities, including drug trafficking, which are worst forms of child labor (section 6, Children).

Also see the Department of Labor's *Findings on the Worst Forms of Child Labor* at www.dol.gov/ilab/reports/child-labor/findings/.

d. Discrimination with Respect to Employment and Occupation

The law and regulations prohibit employment discrimination regarding race, sex, gender, disability, language, sexual orientation and gender identity, HIV-positive status or presence of other communicable diseases, or social status. The government did not always effectively enforce those laws and regulations due to lack of resources and difficulty in identifying when employers' traditional attitudes toward gender identity or sexual orientation resulted in discriminatory employment practices (see also section 6).

The law allows female employees in the public sector to receive two-thirds of their full-time salary for half-time work, provided they have at least one child under 16 or a child with special needs, regardless of age. Qualifying women may apply for the benefit for a three-year period, renewable twice for a maximum of nine years.

Societal and cultural barriers significantly reduced women's participation in the formal labor force, in particular in managerial positions. Women in the private sector earned on average one-quarter less than men for similar work.

e. Acceptable Conditions of Work

The labor code provides for a range of administratively determined minimum wages. In November 2015 the government announced a new monthly minimum wage for a 40-hour workweek for nonagricultural workers of 290 dinars ($127), and a daily minimum wage for agricultural-sector workers of 13 dinars ($5.70). In October 2015 the Ministry of Social Affairs, UGTT, and the Tunisian Union of Agriculture and Fishing reached an agreement to improve labor conditions and salaries in agricultural work to match those in the industrial sector. The agreement allows for the protection of rural women against dangerous employment conditions, sets safety standards for handling of hazardous materials, and gives tax incentives for agricultural employers to provide training for workers.

The law sets a maximum standard 48-hour workweek for manual work in the industrial and agricultural sectors and requires one 24-hour rest period per week. For administrative jobs in the private- and public-sectors, the workweek is 40 hours with 125 percent premium pay for overtime. The law prohibits excessive compulsory overtime. Depending on years of service, employees are statutorily awarded 18 to 23 days of paid vacation annually. Although there is no standard practice for reporting labor code violations, workers have the right to report violations to regional labor inspectors.

Special government regulations control employment in hazardous occupations, such as mining, petroleum engineering, and construction. Workers were free to remove themselves from dangerous situations without jeopardizing their employment, and they could take legal action against employers who retaliated against them for exercising this right. The Ministry of Social Affairs is responsible for enforcing health and safety standards in the workplace. Under the law all workers, including those in the informal sector, are afforded the same occupational safety and health protections. Enforcement of these measures was inadequate, according to UGTT representatives. In addition to enforcing occupational safety and health regulations, regional labor inspectors enforced standards related to hourly wage regulations. The country had 347 labor inspectors who inspected most firms approximately once every two years. The government did not adequately enforce the minimum wage law, particularly in nonunionized sectors of the economy. The prohibition against excessive compulsory overtime was not always enforced.

Working conditions and standards generally were better in export-oriented firms, which were mostly foreign owned, than in those firms producing exclusively for the domestic market. According to World Bank statistics, the informal sector employed more than 54 percent of the total workforce, more than half of which was female. According to the government and NGOs, labor laws did not adequately cover the informal sector, where labor violations were reportedly more prevalent. Temporary contract laborers complained they were not afforded the same protections as permanent employees. There were no major industrial accidents during the year. Credible data on workplace accidents, injuries, and fatalities were not available.